KETO CH
RECIP

CW00520683

Delicious, Fast & Simple Ketogenic Waffles to Lose
Weight with Taste and Maintain Your Keto Diet

Written by

Serena Dunn

Table of contents

Introduction

Chaffles, sometimes known as "cheddar waffles," are a tasty waffle that you can make at home using only eggs and butter instead of grains. They are ideal for staying in ketosis because shredded cheese contains no wheat.

The high flour content in normal waffles adds a lot of carbohydrates, which causes your body to stop using fat as an energy source and start accumulating it as a result of insulin spikes caused by carb consumption.

This healthy snack, which adheres to the ketogenic diet guidelines, will keep you feeling full for a long time because it is heavy in fat and protein, reducing overeating. They are a terrific alternative to bread and are excellent in their simplicity.

You may eat this delectable dish at any time of day; there are numerous combinations of low-carb ketogenic foods to choose from, so you're sure to find one you'll appreciate!

They can be delectable sweet sweets, nutritious breakfast food, or a quick snack, depending on how you serve them; try them in sandiches, pizzas, and French toast varieties!

The Chaffle Maker is the finest option for making them, but you can also create them using a conventional Waffle Maker or even a nonstick saucepan.

Delicious Chaffle Recipes

Garlic Herb Blend Seasoning Chaffles

Cooking: 8 Minutes | Servings: 2

Ingredients

- 1 large organic egg, beaten
- ¼ cup Parmesan cheese, shredded
- ¼ cup Mozzarella cheese, shredded
- ½ tablespoon butter, melted
- 1 teaspoon garlic herb blend seasoning
- Salt, to taste

Directions

1. Preheat a mini waffle iron and then grease it.
2. In a bowl, place all the ingredients and beat until well combined.
3. Place half of the mixture into preheated waffle iron and cook for about 4 minutes or until golden brown.
4. Repeat with the remaining mixture.
5. Serve warm.

Nutrition: Calories: 115, Fat: 8.8g, Carbohydrates: 1.2g, Sugar: 0.2g, Protein: 8g

Basil Chaffles

Cooking: 16 Minutes | Servings: 3

Ingredients

- 2 organic eggs, beaten
- ½ cup Mozzarella cheese, shredded
- 1 tablespoon Parmesan cheese, grated
- 1 teaspoon dried basil, crushed
- Pinch of salt

Directions

1. Preheat a mini waffle iron and then grease it.
2. In a medium bowl, place all ingredients and mix until well combined.
3. Place 1/of the mixture into preheated waffle iron and cook for about 3-4 minutes or until golden brown.
4. Repeat with the remaining mixture.
5. Serve warm.

Nutrition: Calories: 99, Fat: 4.2g, Carbohydrates: 0.4g, Sugar: 0.2g, Protein: 5.7g

Almond Flour Chaffle

Preparation: 5 minutes | Cooking: 20 Minutes | Servings: 2

Ingredients
- 1 large egg
- 1 Tbsp. blanched almond flour
- ¼ tsp. baking powder
- ½ cup shredded Mozzarella cheese

Directions
1. Whisk egg, almond flour, and baking powder together.
2. Stir in Mozzarella and set batter aside.
3. Turn on waffle maker to heat and oil it with cooking spray.
4. Pour half of the batter onto waffle maker and spread it evenly with a spoon.
5. Cooking for 3 minutes, or until it reaches desired doneness.
6. Transfer to a plate and repeat with remaining batter.
7. Let chaffles cool for 2-3 minutes to crisp up.

Nutrition: Calories: 405, Total fat: 38g, Protein: 11g, Total carbs: 10g

Dairy Free and Egg Free Chaffle Bread

Preparation: 1 minute + | Cooking: 3 minutes | Servings: 1

Ingredients

- 3 tbsp almond flour
- 1 tbsp veganaise
- 1/8 tsp baking powder
- 1/4 cup ju.st egg an egg replacer

Directions

1. Add all the ingredients to a small bowl and mix well until it's fully combined.
2. Preheat the waffle maker and add half the mixture to the waffle maker.
3. Cook it for about 3 minutes.
4. Set on a cooling rack.
5. Cook the last bit of batter to make the second piece of bread.

Rosemary Chaffles

Cooking: 8 Minutes | Servings: 2

Ingredients

- 1 organic egg, beaten
- ½ cup Cheddar cheese, shredded
- 1 tablespoon almond flour
- 1 tablespoon fresh rosemary, chopped
- Pinch of salt and freshly ground black pepper

Directions

1. Preheat a mini waffle iron and then grease it.
2. For chaffles: In a medium bowl, place all ingredients and with a fork, mix until well combined.
3. Place half of the mixture into preheated waffle iron and cook for about 4 minutes or until golden brown.
4. Repeat with the remaining mixture.
5. Serve warm.

Nutrition: Calories: 173, Fat: 13.7g, Carbohydrates: 2.2g, Sugar: 0.4g, Protein: 9.9g

Protein Chaffles

Cooking: 4 Minutes | Servings: 1

Ingredients

- ¼ cup almond milk
- ¼ cup plant-based protein powder
- 2 tbsp almond butter
- 1 tbsp psyllium husk

Directions

1. Preheat the waffle maker.
2. Combine almond milk, protein powder, psyllium husk and mix thoroughly until the mixture gets the form of a paste.
3. Add in butter, combine well and form round balls
4. Place the ball in the center of preheated waffle maker.
5. Cook for 4 minutes.
6. Remove, top as prefer and enjoy.

Nutrition: Calories: 310 Kcal ; Fats: 19 g ; Carbs: 5 g ; Protein: 25 g

Onion Chaffle

Preparation: 4 minutes | Cooking: 16 minutes | Servings: 4 chaffles

Ingredients

- 2 eggs
- 1 cup shredded mozzarella cheese
- 1 large sweet onion, rings
- A pinch of salt

Directions

1. Heat up the mini waffle maker.
2. In a small bowl, whisk the egg until beaten and then combine mozzarella cheese and onion. Mix well and add a pinch of salt.
3. Pour ¼ of the batter into the waffle maker and cook for about 4 minutes until golden brown. Repeat with the rest of the batter to make other 3 chaffles.
4. Let cool for 3 minutes to let chaffles get crispy.
5. Serve and enjoy!

Basic Mozzarella Chaffles

Cooking: 6 Minutes | Servings: 2

Ingredients

- 1 large organic egg, beaten
- ½ cup Mozzarella cheese, shredded finely

Directions

1. Preheat a mini waffle iron and then grease it.
2. In a small bowl, place the egg and Mozzarella cheese and stir to combine.
3. Place half of the mixture into preheated waffle iron and cook for about 2-minutes or until golden brown.
4. Repeat with the remaining mixture.
5. Serve warm.

Nutrition: Calories: 5, Net Carb: 0.4g, Fat: 3.7g, Carbohydrates: 0.4g, Sugar: 0.2g, Protein: 5.2g

Cheddar & Almond Flour Chaffles

Preparation: 5 minutes | Cooking: 10 Minutes | Servings: 2

Ingredients

- 1 large organic egg, beaten
- ½ cup Cheddar cheese, shredded
- 2 tablespoons almond flour

Directions

1. Preheat a mini waffle iron and then grease it.
2. In a bowl, place the egg, Cheddar cheese and almond flour and beat until well combined.
3. Place half of the mixture into preheated waffle iron and cook for about 5 minutes or until golden brown.
4. Repeat with the remaining mixture.
5. Serve warm.

Nutrition: Calories: 195, Fat: 15g, Carbohydrates: 1.8g, Sugar: 0.6g, Protein: 10.2g

Dried Herbs Chaffles

Cooking: 8 Minutes | Servings: 2

Ingredients

- 1 organic egg, beaten
- ½ cup Cheddar cheese, shredded
- 1 tablespoon almond flour
- Pinch of dried thyme, crushed
- Pinch of dried rosemary, crushed

Directions

1. Preheat a mini waffle iron and then grease it.
2. In a bowl, place all the ingredients and beat until well combined.
3. Place half of the mixture into preheated waffle iron and cook for about 4 minutes or until golden brown.
4. Repeat with the remaining mixture.
5. Serve warm.

Nutrition: Calories: 112, Fat: 13.4g, Carbohydrates: 1.3g, Sugar: 0.4g, Protein: 9.8g

Garlic Cheese Chaffle Bread Sticks

Preparation: 5 min. | Cooking: 5 min. | Servings: 8

Ingredients

- 1 medium egg
- ½ cup mozzarella cheese, grated
- 2 Tbsp almond flour
- ½ tsp garlic powder
- ½ tsp oregano
- ½ tsp salt

For the toppings

- 2 Tbsp butter, unsalted softened
- ½ tsp garlic powder
- ¼ cup grated mozzarella cheese
- 2 tsp dried oregano for sprinkling

Directions

1. Turn on waffle maker to heat and oil it with cooking spray. Beat egg in a bowl.
2. Add mozzarella, garlic powder, flour, oregano, and salt, and mix.
3. Spoon half of the batter into the waffle maker. Close and cook for 5 minutes. Remove cooked chaffle. Repeat with remaining batter.
4. Place chaffles on a tray and preheat the grill.
5. Mix butter with garlic powder and spread over the chaffles.
6. Sprinkle mozzarella over top and cook under the broiler for 2-3 minutes, until cheese has melted.

Nutrition: Carbs: 1g, Fat: 7 g, Protein: 4g, Calories: 74

Egg-Free Psyllium Husk Chaffles

Preparation: 2 Minutes | Cooking: 4 Minutes | Servings: 1

Ingredients

- 1 ounce Mozzarella cheese, shredded
- 1 tablespoon cream cheese, softened
- 1 tablespoon psyllium husk powder

Directions

1. Preheat a waffle iron and then grease it.
2. In a blender, place all ingredients and pulse until a slightly crumbly mixture forms.
3. Place the mixture into preheated waffle iron and cook for about 4 minutes or until golden brown.
4. Serve warm.

Nutrition: Calories 208, Fat 13.5g, Carbohydrate 0.7g, Protein 8.2g, Sugars 0.6g

Simple Chaffle Toast

Cooking: 5 Minutes | Servings: 2

Ingredients

- 1 large egg
- 1/2 cup shredded cheddar cheese

Toppings:

- 1 egg
- 3-4 spinach leaves
- ¼ cup boil and shredded chicken

Directions

1. Preheat your square waffle maker on medium-high heat.
2. Mix together egg and cheese in a bowl and make two chaffles in a chaffle maker.
3. Once chaffle are cooked, carefully remove them from the maker.
4. Serve with spinach, boiled chicken, and fried egg.
5. Serve hot and enjoy!

Nutrition: Protein: 39% 99 kcal, Fat: % 153 kcal, Carbohydrates: 1% 3 kcal

Keto Sweet Bread Chaffle

Preparation: 10 minutes+ | Cooking: 3 minutes | Servings: 1

Ingredients

- 1 tbs almond flour
- 1 egg
- 1 tbs mayo we love this brand of mayo
- 1/8 tsp baking powder
- 1 tbs Allulose sweetener powdered
- 1/4 tsp cinnamon
- 1/8 tsp salt

Directions

1. Stir all ingredients: together. Let rest for 5 min.
2. Stir again.
3. Preheat the mini waffle iron
4. Put half of dough in mini waffle maker.
5. Cook 3 minutes.
6. Repeat. Let cool.

Nutrition: Calories: 199kcal, Carbohydrates: 3g, Protein: 7g, Fat: 18g, Saturated Fat: 3g , Cholesterol: 169mg, Sodium: 441mg, Potassium: 124mg, Fiber: 1g, Sugar: 1g, Vitamin A: 238IU, Calcium: 66mg

Crispy Chaffles With Egg and Asparagus

Preparation: 15 min | Cooking: 10 min | Servings: 1

Ingredients

- 1 egg
- 1/4 cup cheddar cheese
- 2 tbsps. almond flour
- ½ tsp. baking powder
- 1 egg
- 4-5 stalks asparagus
- 1 tsp. avocado oil

Directions

1. Preheat waffle maker to medium-high heat.
2. Whisk together egg, Mozzarella cheese, almond flour, and baking powder
3. Pour chaffles mixture into the center of the waffle iron. Close the waffle maker and let cooking for 3-5 minutes or until waffle is golden brown and set.
4. Remove chaffles from the waffle maker and serve.
5. Meanwhile, heat oil in a nonstick pan.
6. Once the pan is hot, fry asparagus for about 4-5 minutes until golden brown.
7. Poach the egg in boil water for about 2-3 minutes.
8. Once chaffles are cooked, remove from the maker.
9. Serve chaffles with the poached egg and asparagus.

Nutrition: Calories: 287 kcal, Total Fat: 19g, Total Carbs: 6.5g, Protein: 6.8g

Cheddar & Egg White Chaffles

Cooking: 12 Minutes | Servings: 4

Ingredients

- 2 egg whites
- 1 cup Cheddar cheese, shredded

Directions

1. Preheat a mini waffle iron and then grease it.
2. In a small bowl, place the egg whites and cheese and stir to combine.
3. Place ¼ of the mixture into preheated waffle iron and cook for about 4 minutes or until golden brown.
4. Repeat with the remaining mixture. Serve warm.

Nutrition: Calories: 122, Net Carb: 0.5g, Fat: 9.4g, Carbohydrates: 0.5g, Dietary Fiber: 0g, Sugar: 0.3g, Protein: 8.8g

Broccoli Plus Cheese Chaffle

Preparation: 2 minutes | Cooking: 8 minutes | Servings: 2

Ingredients
- 1/2 cup cheddar cheese
- 1/4 cup fresh chopped broccoli
- 1 egg
- 1/4 teaspoon garlic powder
- 1 tablespoon almond flour

Directions
1. In a bowl, mix almond flour, cheddar cheese, egg, and garlic powder. I find it easiest to mix everything using a fork.
2. Add half the Broccoli and Cheese Chaffle batter to the Dish Mini waffle maker at a time.
3. Cooking chaffle batter in the waffle maker for 4 minutes.
4. Let each chaffle sit for 1-2 minutes on a plate to firm up. Enjoy alone or dipping in sour cream or ranch dressing.

Nutrition: Calories 502, Fat 26, Carbs 13, Protein 27

Avocado Croque Madam Chaffle

Preparation: 10 minutes | Cooking: 15 minutes | Servings: 4

Ingredients
- 4 eggs
- 2 cups grated Mozzarella cheese
- 1 avocado, mashed
- Salt and pepper to taste
- 6 tablespoons almond flour
- 2 teaspoons baking powder
- 1 teaspoon dried dill
- 2 tablespoons cooking spray to brush the waffle maker
- 4 fried eggs
- 2 tablespoons freshly chopped basil

Directions
1. Preheat the waffle maker.
2. Add the eggs, grated mozzarella, avocado, salt and pepper, almond flour, baking powder and dried dill to a bowl.
3. Mix with a fork.
4. Brush the heated waffle maker with cooking spray and add a few tablespoons of the batter.
5. Close the lid and cooking for about 7 minutes depending on your waffle maker.
6. Serve each chaffle with a fried egg and freshly chopped basil on top.

Nutrition: Calories 304, Fat 24.9, Fiber 5.4, Carbs 6.5, Protein 13.8

Fruity Vegan Chaffles

Preparation: 10 minutes | Cooking: 5 minutes | Servings: 2

Ingredients

- 1 tbsp. chia seeds
- 2 tbsps. warm water
- ¼ cup low carb vegan cheese
- 2 tbsps. strawberry puree
- 2 tbsps. Greek yogurt
- pinch of salt

Directions

1. Preheat waffle maker to medium-high heat.
2. In a small bowl, mix together chia seeds and water and let it stand for few minutes to be thickened.
3. Mix the rest of the ingredients in chia seed egg and mix well.
4. Spray waffle machine with cooking spray.
5. Pour vegan waffle batter into the center of the waffle iron.
6. Close the waffle maker and cooking chaffles for about 3-5 minutes.
7. Once cooked, remove from the maker and serve with berries on top.

Nutrition: 235 Calories, 33.7g Protein, 3.8g Carbohydrates, 8.8g Fat, 0.7g Fiber, 98mg Cholesterol, 778mg Sodium, 604mg Potassium

Salmon Chaffles

Cooking: 10 Minutes | Servings: 2

Ingredients

- 1 large egg
- 1/2 cup shredded mozzarella
- 1 Tbsp cream cheese
- 2 slices salmon
- 1 Tbsp everything bagel seasoning

Directions

1. Turn on waffle maker to heat and oil it with cooking spray.
2. Beat egg in a bowl, then add 1/2 cup of mozzarella.
3. Pour half of the mixture into maker and cook for 4 minutes.
4. Remove and repeat with remaining mixture.
5. Let chaffles cool, then spread cream cheese, sprinkle with seasoning, and top with salmon.

Nutrition: Carbs: 3 g; Fat: 10 g; Protein: 5 g; Calories: 201

Chaffle Katsu Sandwich

Cooking: 20 Minutes | Servings: 4

Ingredients

For the chicken:

- 1/4 lb boneless and skinless thigh
- 1/8 tsp salt
- 1/8 tsp black pepper
- 1/2 cup almond flour
- 1 egg
- 3 oz unflavored pork rinds
- 2 cup vegetable oil for deep frying

For the brine:

- 2 cups of water
- 1 Tbsp salt

For the sauce:

- 2 Tbsp sugar-free ketchup
- 1.1/2 Tbsp Worcestershire Sauce
- 1 Tbsp oyster sauce
- 1 tsp swerve/monkfruit

For the chaffle:

- 2 egg
- 1 cup shredded mozzarella cheese

Directions

1. Add brine Ingredients in a large mixing bowl.
2. Add chicken and brine for 1 hour.

3. Pat chicken dry with a paper towel. Sprinkle with salt and pepper. Set aside.
4. Mix ketchup, oyster sauce, Worcestershire sauce, and swerve in a small bowl.
5. Pulse pork rinds in a food processor making fine crumbs.
6. Fill one bowl with flour, a second bowl with beaten eggs, and a third with, crushed pork rinds.
7. Dip and coat each thigh in: flour, eggs, crushed pork rinds. Transfer on holding 1 a plate.
8. Add oil to cover 1/2 inch of frying pan, Heat to 375 ° F.
9. Once oil is hot, reduce heat to medium and add chicken. Cooking time depends on the chicken thickness
10. Transfer to a drying rack.
11. Turn on waffle maker to heat and oil it with cooking spray.
12. Beat egg in a small bowl.
13. Place 1/8 cup of cheese on waffle maker, then add 4 of the egg mixtures and top with 1/8 cup of cheese.
14. Cook for 3 -4 minutes.
15. Repeat tor remaining batter.
16. Top chaffles with chicken katsu, 1 Tbsp sauce, and another piece of chaffle.

Nutrition: Carbs: 12 g ;Fat: 1 g ;Protein: 2 g; Calories: 5

Keto Chaffe Breakfast Sandwich

| Preparation: 3 minutes+ | Cooking: 10 minutes | Servings: 1

Ingredients

- 1 egg
- 1/2 cup Cheddar cheese, shredded

For the sandwich:

- 2 strips bacon
- 1 egg
- 1 slice Cheddar or American cheese.

Directions

1. Preheat the waffle maker according to manufacturer Directions.
2. In a small mixing bowl, mix together egg and shredded cheese. Stir until well combined.
3. Pour one half of the waffle batter into the waffle maker. Cook for 3-4 minutes or until golden brown. Repeat with the second half of the batter.
4. In a large pan over medium heat, cook the bacon until crispy, turning as needed. Remove to drain on paper towels.
5. In the same skillet, in 1 tbsp of reserved bacon drippings, fry the egg over medium heat. Cook until desired doneness.
6. Assemble the sandwich, and enjoy!

Nutrition: Calories: 658, Total Fat: 51g, Saturated Fat: 25g, Trans Fat: 1g. Unsaturated Fat: 21g, Cholesterol: 495mg, Sodium: 1356mg, Carbohydrates: 6g, Fiber: 0g, Sugar: 2g, Protein: 43g

Chicken & Bacon Chaffles

Cooking: 8 Minutes | Servings: 2

Ingredients

- 1 organic egg, beaten
- 1/3 cup grass-fed cooked chicken, chopped
- 1 cooked bacon slice, crumbled
- 1/3 cup Pepper Jack cheese, shredded
- 1 teaspoon powdered ranch dressing

Directions

1. Preheat a mini waffle iron and then grease it.
2. In a medium bowl, place all ingredients and with a fork, mix until well combined.
3. Place half of the mixture into preheated waffle iron and cook for about 4 minutes or until golden brown.
4. Repeat with the remaining mixture.
5. Serve warm.

Nutrition: Calories: 145, Fat: 9.4g, Carbohydrates: 1g, Sugar: 0.2g, Protein: 14.3g

Pork Rind Chaffles

Cooking: 10 Minutes | Servings: 2

Ingredients

- 1 organic egg, beaten
- ½ cup ground pork rinds
- 1/3 cup Mozzarella cheese, shredded
- Pinch of salt

Directions

1. Preheat a mini waffle iron and then grease it.
2. In a bowl, place all the ingredients and beat until well combined.
3. Place half of the mixture into preheated waffle iron and cook for about 5 minutes or until golden brown.
4. Repeat with the remaining mixture.
5. Serve warm.

Nutrition: Calories: 91, Fat: 5.9g, Carbohydrates: 0.3g, Sugar: 0.2g, Protein: 9.2g

Chicken & Veggies Chaffles

Cooking: 15 Minutes | Servings: 3

Ingredients

- 1/3 cup cooked grass-fed chicken, chopped
- 1/3 cup cooked spinach, chopped
- 1/3 cup marinated artichokes, chopped
- 1 organic egg, beaten
- 1/3 cup Mozzarella cheese, shredded
- 1 ounce cream cheese, softened
- ¼ teaspoon garlic powder

Directions

1. Preheat a mini waffle iron and then grease it.
2. In a medium bowl, place all ingredients and mix until well combined.
3. Place 1/of the mixture into preheated waffle iron and cook for about 4-5 minutes or until golden brown.
4. Repeat with the remaining mixture.
5. Serve warm.

Nutrition: Calories: 95, Fat: 5.8g, Carbohydrates: 2.2g, Sugar: 0.3g, Protein: 8g

Protein Cheddar Chaffles

Cooking: 48 Minutes | Servings: 8

Ingredients

- ½ cup golden flax seeds meal
- ½ cup almond flour
- 2 tablespoons unflavored whey protein powder
- 1 teaspoon organic baking powder
- Salt and ground black pepper, to taste
- ¾ cup cheddar cheese, shredded
- 1/3 cup unsweetened almond milk
- 2 tablespoons unsalted butter, melted
- 2 large organic eggs, beaten

Directions

1. Preheat a mini waffle iron and then grease it.
2. In a large bowl, add flax seeds meal, flour, protein powder, and baking powder, and mix well.
3. Stir in the cheddar cheese.
4. In another bowl, add the remaining ingredients and beat until well combined.
5. Add the egg mixture into the bowl with flax seeds meal mixture and mix until well combined.
6. Place desired amount of the mixture into preheated waffle iron.
7. Cook for about 4-6 minutes.
8. Repeat with the remaining mixture.
9. Serve warm.

Nutrition: Calories 187, Fat 14.5 g, Carbs 4.9 g, Sugar 0.4 g, Protein 8 g

---

Pork Sandwich Chaffles

Preparation: 10 minutes | Cooking: 16 Minutes | Servings: 4

Ingredients

Chaffles:

- 2 large organic eggs
- ¼ cup superfine blanched almond flour ¾ teaspoon organic baking powder ½ teaspoon garlic powder
- 1 cup cheddar cheese, shredded

Filling:

- 12 ounces cooked pork, cut into slices
- 1 tomato, sliced
- 4 lettuce leaves

Directions

1. Preheat a mini waffle iron and then grease it.
2. For chaffles: in a bowl, add the eggs, almond flour, baking powder, and garlic powder, and beat until well combined.
3. Add the cheese and stir to combine.
4. Place ¼ of the mixture into preheated waffle iron and cooking for about 3-minutes.
5. Repeat with the remaining mixture.
6. Serve each chaffle with filling ingredients.

Nutrition: Calories 139, Fat 4.6., Fiber 2.5, Carbs 3.3, Protein 3.5

Cauliflower Chaffles & Tomatoes

Preparation: 5 minutes | Cooking: 10 minutes | Servings: 2

Ingredients

Chaffle:

- Cauliflower (.5 cup)
- Black pepper and salt (.25 tsp. each)
- Garlic powder (.25 tsp.)
- Shredded cheddar cheese (.5 cup)
- Egg (1)

The Topping:

- Sliced tomato (1)
- Lettuce leaves (1)
- Steamed - mashed cauliflower (4 oz.)
- Sesame seeds (1 tsp.)

Directions

1. Toss each of the chaffle ingredients in a blender and thoroughly mix.
2. Warm the waffle maker ahead of cooking time.
3. Drizzle ⅛ teaspoon of shredded cheese over the waffle iron grids.
4. Pour in the mixture and add the rest of the cheese.
5. Prepare the chaffles for four to five minutes.
6. Serve with a chaffle, lettuce leaf, and tomato, cauliflower, with a topping of seeds.

Nutrition: Calories: 198, Net Carbohydrates: 1.73 grams, Protein: 12.74 grams, Fats: 14.34 grams

Scallion - Coconut Chaffles

Preparation: 5 minutes | Cooking: 10 minutes | Servings: 2

Ingredients

- Shredded mozzarella cheese (1 cup)
- Egg (1)
- Cheddar cheese - shredded (1 cup)
- Coconut flour (1.5 tsp.)
- Sliced scallions (2 tbsp.)
- Salt and black pepper (to taste)

Directions

1. Heat a mini waffle maker and spray it using a cooking oil spray.
2. Toss each of the fixings into a bowl and whisk thoroughly.
3. Prepare the batter in two batches, cooking until nicely browned, and serve them right from the cooker.

Nutrition: Calories: 346, Net Carbohydrates: 7.9 grams, Protein: 22.6 grams, Fats: 25 grams

Mushrooms Pizza Chaffle

Preparation: 5 minutes | Cooking: 10 minutes | Servings: 2 chaffles

Ingredients

For chaffles:

- ½ cup shredded mozzarella cheese
- 1 tbsp almond flour
- ½ tsp baking powder
- 1 egg, beaten
- A pinch of salt

For topping:

- 2 tbsp low carb pasta sauce
- 2 tbsp mozzarella cheese, shredded
- 1 can mushrooms, drained
- 1 tsp dried oregano

Directions

1. Heat up the waffle maker.
2. Add all the chaffle ingredients to a small mixing bowl and combine well.
3. Pour down half of the batter into the waffle maker and cook for about 4 minutes until golden brown color. Repeat with the rest of the batter to make another chaffle.
4. Once both chaffles are cooked, place them on the baking sheet of the toaster oven.
5. Put 1 tbsp of low carb pasta sauce on top of each chaffle.

---

6. Sprinkle 1 tbsp of shredded mozzarella cheese on top of each one.
7. Top with mushrooms and sprinkle with oregano.
8. Bake it at 350° in the toaster oven for about 2 minutes, until the cheese is melted.
9. Serve and enjoy!

Parmesan Pizza Chaffle

Preparation: 5 minutes | Cooking: 13 minutes | Servings: 2 chaffles

Ingredients

For chaffles:

- ½ cup shredded mozzarella cheese
- 1 tbsp almond flour
- ½ tsp baking powder
- 1 egg, beaten
- ¼ tsp garlic powder
- A pinch of salt and pepper

For pizza topping:

- 2 tbsp low carb pasta sauce
- 2 tbsp mozzarella cheese, shredded
- 1 tbsp parmesan cheese, shredded
- ¼ tsp fresh basil

Directions

1. Heat up the waffle maker.
2. Add all the chaffle ingredients to a small mixing bowl and combine well.
3. Pour down half of the batter into the waffle maker and cook for about 4 minutes until golden brown color. Repeat with the rest of the batter to make another chaffle.
4. Once both chaffles are cooked, place them on the baking sheet of the toaster oven.
5. Put 1 tbsp of low carb pasta sauce on top of each chaffle.

6. Sprinkle 1 tbsp of shredded mozzarella and 1 tbsp of shredded parmesan on top of each one. Season with fresh basil.
7. Bake it at 350° in the toaster oven for about 5 minutes, until the cheese is melted.
8. Serve and enjoy!

Garlic and Onion Powder Chaffles

Preparation: 5 minutes | Cooking: 5 Minutes | Servings: 2

Ingredients

- 1 organic egg, beaten
- ¼ cup Cheddar cheese, shredded
- 2 tablespoons almond flour
- ½ teaspoon organic baking powder
- ¼ teaspoon garlic powder
- ¼ teaspoon onion powder
- Pinch of salt

Directions

1. Preheat a waffle iron and then grease it.
2. In a bowl, place all the ingredients and beat until well combined.
3. Place the mixture into preheated waffle iron and cook for about 5 minutes or until golden brown.
4. Serve warm.

Nutrition: Calories 249, Protein 12 g, Carbs 30 g, Fat 10 g, Sodium (Na) 32 mg, Potassium (K) 398 mg, Phosphorus 190 mg

Cheese Garlic Chaffle

Preparation: 10 minutes | Cooking: 8 Minutes | Servings: 2

Ingredients

Chaffle:

- 1 egg
- 1 teaspoon cream cheese
- ½ cup mozzarella cheese, shredded
- ½ teaspoon garlic powder
- 1 teaspoon Italian seasoning

Topping:

- 1 tablespoon butter
- ½ teaspoon garlic powder
- ½ teaspoon Italian seasoning
- 2 tablespoon mozzarella cheese, shredded

Directions:

1. Plug in your waffle maker to preheat.
2. Preheat your oven to 350 degrees F.
3. In a bowl, combine all the chaffle ingredients.
4. Cook in the waffle maker for minutes per chaffle.
5. Transfer to a baking pan.
6. Spread butter on top of each chaffle.
7. Sprinkle garlic powder and Italian seasoning on top.
8. Top with mozzarella cheese.
9. Bake until the cheese has melted.

Nutrition: Calories 526, Fat 53.2, Fiber 7.8, Carbs 11.7, Protein 8.2

Egg & Chives Chaffle Sandwich Roll

Preparation: 10 minutes | Cooking: 0 Minute | Servings: 2

Ingredients

- 2 tablespoons mayonnaise
- 1 hard-boiled egg, chopped
- 1 tablespoon chives, chopped
- 2 basic chaffles (Choose 1 Recipe From Chapter 1)

Directions

1. In a bowl, mix the mayo, egg and chives.
2. Spread the mixture on top of the chaffles.
3. Roll the chaffle.

Nutrition: Calories 256, Total Fat 20g, Saturated Fat 4g, Total Carbs 11g, Net Carbs 5g, Protein 8g, Sugar: 9g, Fiber: 6g

Cinnamon Chaffle Rolls

Preparation: 7 minutes | Cooking: 10 Minutes | Servings: 2

Ingredients

- 1/2 cup mozzarella cheese
- 1 tbsp. almond flour
- 1 egg
- 1 tsp cinnamon
- 1 tsp stevia

Cinnamon Roll Glaze:

- 1 tbsp. butter
- 1 tbsp. cream cheese
- 1 tsp. cinnamon
- 1/4 tsp vanilla extract
- 1 tbsp. coconut flour

Directions

1. Switch on a round waffle maker and let it heat up.
2. In a small bowl mix together cheese, egg, flour, cinnamon powder, and stevia in a bowl.
3. Spray the round waffle maker with nonstick spray.
4. Pour the batter in a waffle maker and close the lid.
5. Close the waffle maker and cook for about 3-4 minutes.
6. Once chaffles are cooked, remove from Maker
7. Mix together butter, cream cheese, cinnamon, vanilla and coconut flour in a bowl.
8. Spread this glaze over chaffle and roll up.
9. Serve and enjoy!

Nutrition: Calories 176, Fat 2.1g, Carbs 27g, Protein 15.1g, Potassium (K) 242mg, Sodium (Na) 72mg, Phosphorous 555.3 mg

Taco Chaffles

Preparation: 10 minutes | Cooking: 20 Minutes | Servings: 2

Ingredients

- 1 tablespoon almond flour
- 1 cup taco blend cheese
- 2 organic eggs
- ¼ teaspoon taco seasoning

Directions

1. Preheat a mini waffle iron and then grease it.
2. In a bowl, place all ingredients and mix until well combined.
3. Place ¼ of the mixture into preheated waffle iron and cook for about 4 minutes or until golden brown.
4. Repeat with the remaining mixture.
5. Serve warm.

Nutrition: Calories 221, Protein 14 g, Carbs 3 g, Fat 2 g, Sodium (Na) 119 mg, Potassium (K) 398 mg, Phosphorus 149 mg

Zucchini Chaffles With Peanut Butter

Preparation: 5 minutes | Cooking: 5 Minutes | Servings: 2

Ingredients

- 1 cup zucchini grated
- 1 egg beaten
- 1/2 cup shredded parmesan cheese
- 1/4 cup shredded mozzarella cheese
- 1 tsp dried basil
- 1/2 tsp. salt
- 1/2 tsp. black pepper
- 2 tbsps. peanut butter for topping

Directions

1. Sprinkle salt over zucchini and let it sit for minutes.
2. Squeeze out water from zucchini.
3. Beat egg with zucchini, basil. salt mozzarella cheese, and pepper.
4. Sprinkle ½ of the parmesan cheese over preheated waffle maker and pour zucchini batter over it.
5. Sprinkle the remaining cheese over it.
6. Close the lid.
7. Cook zucchini chaffles for about 4-8 minutes Utes.
8. Remove chaffles from the maker and repeat with the remaining batter.
9. Serve with peanut butter on top and enjoy!

Nutrition: Calories 124, Protein 15 g, Carbs 0 g, Fat 7 g, Sodium (Na) 161 mg, Potassium (K) 251 mg, Phosphorus 220 mg

Blueberry Chaffles

Preparation: 8 minutes | Cooking: 15 Minutes | Servings: 2

Ingredients

- 2 eggs
- 1/2 cup blueberries
- 1/2 tsp baking powder
- 1/2 tsp vanilla
- 2 tsp Swerve
- 3 tbsp almond flour
- 1 cup mozzarella cheese, shredded

Directions

1. Preheat your waffle maker.
2. In a medium bowl, mix eggs, vanilla, Swerve, almond flour, and cheese.
3. Add blueberries and stir well.
4. Spray waffle maker with cooking spray.
5. Pour 1/4 batter in the hot waffle maker and cook for 8 minutes or until golden brown. Repeat with the remaining batter.
6. Serve and enjoy.

Nutrition: Calories 96, Fat 6.1g, Carbohydrates 5g, Sugar 2.2g, Protein 6.1g, Cholesterol 86 mg

Vegetarian Chaffle Sandwich

Cooking: 8 Minutes | Servings: 2

Ingredients

Chaffle:

- 1 large egg (beaten)
- 1/8 tsp onion powder
- 1 tbsp almond flour
- 1/2 cup shredded mozzarella cheese
- 1 tsp nutmeg
- 1/4 tsp baking powder

Sandwich Filling:

- 1/2 cup shredded carrot
- 1/2 cup sliced cucumber
- 1/2 medium bell pepper (sliced)
- 1 cup mixed salad greens
- 1/2 avocado (mashed and divided)
- 6 tbsp keto friendly hummus

Directions

For the chaffle:

1. Plug the waffle maker to preheat it. Spray it with non-stick cooking spray.
2. Combine the baking powder, nutmeg, flour and onion powder in a mixing bowl. Add the eggs and mix.
3. Add the cheese and mix until the ingredients are well combined and you have formed a smooth batter.

---

4. Pour the batter into the waffle maker and spread it out to the edges of the waffle maker to cover all the holes on it.
5. Close the waffle lid and cook for about 5 minutes or according to waffle maker's settings.
6. After the cooking cycle, remove the chaffle from the waffle maker with a plastic or silicone utensil.

For the sandwich:

7. Add 3 tablespoons of hummus to one chaffle and spread with a spoon.
8. Fill another chaffle with one half of the mashed avocado.
9. Fill the first chaffle slice with 1/4 cup sliced cucumber, 1/2 cup mixed salad greens, 1/4 cup shredded carrot and
10. one half of the sliced bell pepper.
11. Place the chaffle on top and press lightly.
12. Repeat step 7 to 10 for the remaining ingredients to make the second sandwich.
13. Serve and enjoy.

Nutrition: Fat 22g 28%, Carbohydrate 17.8g 6%, Sugars 4.6g, Protein 11.3g

Club Sandwich Chaffles

Preparation: 4 minutes | Cooking: 16 minutes | Servings: 4 chaffles

Ingredients

For chaffles:

- 2 eggs, beaten
- 1 cup shredded cheddar cheese

For club sandwich:

- 2 Iceberg lettuce leaves
- 2 tsp keto mayonnaise
- 2 slices of deli ham
- 2 slices deli turkey
- 2 sliced cheddar cheese
- 1 small tomato, sliced
- 2 slices of bacon, cooked

Directions

1. Heat up the waffle maker.
2. Add egg and shredded cheese to a small mixing bowl and combine well.
3. Pour ¼ of the batter into the waffle maker and cook for 4 minutes until golden brown. Repeat with the rest of the batter to prepare the other chaffles.
4. Let cool for 3 minutes to let chaffles get crispy. You need 3 chaffles for this sandwich.
5. Spread the chaffle with keto mayonnaise. Top with lettuce leaves, 1 slice of deli ham, 1 slice of deli turkey, 1 slice of cheddar cheese, 1 slice of tomato, 1

slice of bacon. Cover with another chaffle and repeat the procedure. Cover with the 3rd chaffle.

6. Serve and enjoy!

Chaffles Sandwich Deli Ham, Brie & Avocado

Preparation: 5 minutes | Cooking: 8 minutes | Servings: 2 chaffles

Ingredients

For the chaffles:

- ½ cup cheddar cheese, grated
- 1 large egg, beaten
- A pinch of salt

For filling:

- 1 slice of deli ham
- 1 small avocado, thinly sliced
- 1 slice of Brie cheese, very thin
- 1 tsp sesame seeds
- 1 tbsp keto mayonnaise

Directions

1. Heat up the waffle maker.
2. Add all the chaffles ingredients to a mixing bowl. Stir until well combined.
3. Pour half of the batter into the waffle maker and cook for 4 minutes until golden brown. Repeat with the rest of the batter to make another chaffle.
4. Spread the chaffle with mayonnaise; top with a slice of deli ham, a slice of Brie, a few slices of avocado. Sprinkle with sesame seeds. Cover with another chaffle.
5. Serve and enjoy!

Vegetables Chaffles Sandwich

Preparation: 5 minutes | Cooking: 8 minutes | Servings: 2 chaffles

Ingredients

For chaffles:

- 1 large egg, beaten
- ½ cup of mozzarella cheese, shredded

For filling:

- 1 tbsp butter, unsalted
- 1 slice of Fontina cheese
- 2 slices of grilled onions
- 2 slices of grilled zucchinis
- 1 slice of grilled bell pepper

Directions:

1. Heat up the waffle maker.
2. Add all the chaffles ingredients to a small mixing bowl and stir until well combined.
3. Pour half of the batter into the waffle maker and cook for 4 minutes until golden brown. Repeat with the rest of the batter to make another chaffle.
4. Spread the butter on the chaffle. Top it with a slice of Fontina cheese, onions, zucchinis and bell peppers. Cover with another chaffle.
5. Serve and enjoy!

Pork Tenderloin Chaffles Sandwich

Preparation: 5 minutes | Cooking: 8 minutes | Servings: 2 chaffles

Ingredients

For chaffles:

- 1 large egg, beaten
- ½ cup of Mozzarella cheese, shredded

For filling:

- 1 thin slice of cooked pork tenderloin
- Lettuce leaves
- 1 small tomato, sliced
- 1 tbsp keto mayonnaise
- A pinch of black pepper

Directions

1. Heat up the waffle maker.
2. Add all the chaffles ingredients to a small mixing bowl and combine well.
3. Pour half of the batter into the waffle maker and cook for 4 minutes until golden brown. Repeat with the rest of the batter to make another chaffle.
4. Spread the chaffle with mayonnaise and top with a slice of pork tenderloin, tomato and lettuce. Season with black pepper to taste. Cover with another chaffle.
5. Serve warm and enjoy!

Jalapeno & Bacon Chaffle

Preparation: 5 minutes | Cooking: 5 minutes | Servings: 6

Ingredients

- 3 tbsp. coconut flour
- 1 tsp. baking powder
- 3 eggs
- 8 oz. cream cheese
- ¼ tsp. salt
- 4 bacon slices
- 2 to 3 jalapenos
- 1 cup cheddar cheese

Directions

1. Wash the jalapeno and slice them.
2. Take a pan and cooking jalapeno until golden brown or crispy.
3. Take a bowl add flour, baking powder and salt and mix.
4. In a mixing bowl add cream and beat well until fluffy.
5. Now in another bowl add egg and whisk them well.
6. Pour cream, cheese and beat until well combined.
7. Add the mixture with dry ingredients and make a smooth batter. After that fold the jalapeno in mixture.
8. Heat the waffle maker and pour the batter into it.
9. Cooking it for 5 minutes or until golden brown.
10. Top it with cheese, jalapeno and crème and serve the hot chaffles.

Nutrition: Net Carbs: 2.8g; Calories: 310; Total Fat: 20g; Saturated Fat: 4.8g; Protein: 30.2g; Carbs: 3.1g; Fiber: 0.3g; Sugar: 1.2g

Crispy Chaffles With Sausage

Cooking: 10 Minutes | Servings: 2

Ingredients

- 1/2 cup cheddar cheese
- 1/2 tsp. baking powder
- 1/4 cup egg whites
- 2 tsp. pumpkin spice

For Serving:

- 1 egg, whole
- 2 chicken sausage
- 2 slice bacon
- salt and pepper to taste
- 1 tsp. avocado oil

Directions:

1. Mix together all ingredients in a bowl.
2. Allow batter to sit while waffle iron warms.
3. Spray waffle iron with nonstick spray.
4. Pour batter in the waffle maker and cook according to the directions of the manufacturer.
5. Meanwhile, heat oil in a pan and fry the egg, according to your choice and transfer it toa plate.
6. In the same pan, fry bacon slice and sausage on medium heat for about 2-3 minutes until cooked.
7. Once chaffles are cooked thoroughly, remove them from the maker.
8. Serve with fried egg, bacon slice, sausages and enjoy!

Nutrition: Protein: 22% 86 kcal Fat: 74% 286 kcal
Carbohydrates: 3% 12 kcal

Bacon & 3-cheese Chaffles

Preparation: 10 minutes | Cooking: 8 Minutes | Servings: 2

Ingredients

- 3 large organic eggs
- ½ cup Swiss cheese, grated
- 1/3 cup Parmesan cheese, grated
- 1/4 cup cream cheese, softened
- 4 tablespoons almond flour
- 1 tablespoon coconut flour
- ½ teaspoon onion powder
- ½ teaspoon garlic powder
- ½ teaspoon dried basil, crushed
- ½ teaspoon dried oregano, crushed
- ½ teaspoon organic baking powder
- Salt and freshly ground black pepper, to taste
- 4 cooked bacon slices, cut in half

Directions

- Preheat a waffle iron and then grease it.
- In a bowl, place all the ingredients except for bacon and mix until well combined.
- Place ¼ of the mixture into preheated waffle iron.
- Arrange 2 halved bacon slices over mixture and cook for about 2 minutes or until golden brown.
- Repeat with the remaining mixture and bacon slices.
- Serve warm.

Nutrition: Calories 61, Fat 2.3, Fiber 4, Carbs 10.7, Protein 1.4

Bacon Chaffle

Cooking: 7–9 Minutes | Servings: 4

Ingredients

Batter:

- 4 eggs
- 2 cups shredded mozzarella
- 2 ounces finely chopped bacon
- Salt and pepper to taste
- 1 teaspoon dried oregano

Other:

- 2 tablespoons olive oil for brushing the waffle maker

Directions

1. Preheat the waffle maker.
2. Crack the eggs into a bowl and add the grated mozzarella cheese.
3. Mix until just combined and stir in the chopped bacon.
4. Season with salt and pepper and dried oregano.
5. Brush the heated waffle maker with olive oil and add a few tablespoons of the batter.
6. Close the lid and cook for about 7–8 minutes depending on your waffle maker.

Nutrition: Calories 241, fat 19.8 g, carbs 1.3 g, sugar 0.4 g, Protein 14.8 g, sodium 4 mg

Blue Cheese Chaffle Bites

Cooking: 14 Minutes| Servings: 2

Ingredients

- 1 egg, beaten
- ½ cup finely grated Parmesan cheese
- ¼ cup crumbled blue cheese
- 1 tsp erythritol

Directions

- Preheat the waffle iron.
- Mix all the Ingredients in a bowl.
- Open the iron and add half of the mixture.
- Close and cook until crispy, 7 minutes.
- Remove the chaffle onto a plate and make another with the remaining mixture.
- Cut each chaffle into wedges and serve afterward.

Nutrition: Calories 19ats 13.91gCarbs 4.03gNet Carbs 4.03gProtein 13.48g

Mayonnaise & Cream Cheese Chaffles

Cooking: 20 Minutes | Servings: 4

Ingredients
- 4 organic eggs large
- 4 tablespoons mayonnaise
- 1 tablespoon almond flour
- 2 tablespoons cream cheese, cut into small cubes

Directions
1. Preheat a waffle iron and then grease it.
2. In a bowl, place the eggs, mayonnaise and almond flour and with a hand mixer, mix until smooth.
3. Place about ¼ of the mixture into preheated waffle iron.
4. Place about ¼ of the cream cheese cubes on top of the mixture evenly and cook for about 5 minutes or until golden brown.
5. Repeat with the remaining mixture and cream cheese cubes. Serve warm.

Nutrition: Calories: 190, Net Carb: 0.6g, Fat: 17g, Saturated Fat: 4.2g, Carbohydrates: 0.8g, Dietary Fiber: 0.2g, Sugar: 0.5g, Protein: 6.7g

Egg-free Coconut Flour Chaffles

Cooking: 10 Minutes | Servings: 2

Ingredients
- 1 tablespoon flaxseed meal
- 2½ tablespoons water
- ¼ cup Mozzarella cheese, shredded
- 1 tablespoon cream cheese, softened
- 2 tablespoons coconut flour

Directions
1. Preheat a waffle iron and then grease it.
2. In a bowl, place the flaxseed meal and water and mix well.
3. Set aside for about 5 minutes or until thickened.
4. In the bowl of flaxseed mixture, add the remaining ingredients and mix until well combined.
5. Place half of the mixture into preheated waffle iron and cook for about 3-minutes or until golden brown.
6. Repeat with the remaining mixture. Serve warm.

Nutrition: Calories: 76, Net Carb: 2.3g, Fat: 4.2g, Saturated Fat: 2.1g, Carbohydrates: 6.3g, Dietary Fiber: 4g, Sugar: 0.1g, Protein: 3g

Cajun & Feta Chaffle

Preparation: 10 minutes | Cooking: 10 Minutes | Servings: 1

Ingredients

- 1 egg white
- 1/4 cup shredded mozzarella cheese
- 2 tbsps. almond flour
- 1 tsp Cajun Seasoning

For Serving:

- 1 egg
- 4 oz. feta cheese
- 1 tomato, sliced

Directions

1. Whisk together egg, cheese, and seasoning in a bowl.
2. Switch on and grease waffle maker with cooking spray.
3. Pour batter in a preheated waffle maker.
4. Cook chaffles for about 2-3 minutes until the chaffle is cooked through.
5. Meanwhile, fry the egg in a non-stick pan for about 1-2 minutes.
6. For serving set fried egg on chaffles with feta cheese and tomatoes slice.

Nutrition: Protein: 28% 119 kcal, Fat: 64% 2 kcal, Carbohydrates: 7% 31 kcal

Breakfast Bacon Chaffles

Preparation: 10 minutes | Cooking: 7–9 Minutes | Servings: 4

Ingredients:

Batter:

- 4 eggs
- 2 cups shredded mozzarella
- 2 ounces finely chopped bacon
- Salt and pepper to taste
- 1 teaspoon dried oregano

Other:

- 2 tablespoons olive oil for brushing the waffle maker

Directions

1. Preheat the waffle maker.
2. Crack the eggs into a bowl and add the grated mozzarella cheese.
3. Mix until just combined and stir in the chopped bacon.
4. Season with salt and pepper and dried oregano.
5. Brush the heated waffle maker with olive oil and add a few tablespoons of the batter.
6. Close the lid and cook for about 7–8 minutes depending on your waffle maker.

Nutrition: Calories 241, fat 19.8 g, carbs 1.3 g, sugar 0.4 g, Protein 14.8 g, sodium 4 mg

Chaffles Bowl

Preparation: 10 minutes | Cooking: 5 Minutes | Servings: 2

Ingredients
- 1 egg
- 1/2 cup cheddar cheese shredded
- pinch of Italian seasoning
- 1 tbsp. pizza sauce

Topping:
- 1/2 avocado sliced
- 2 eggs boiled
- 1 tomato, halves
- 4 oz. fresh spinach leaves

Directions
1. Preheat your waffle maker and grease with cooking spray.
2. Crack an egg in a small bowl and beat with Italian seasoning and pizza sauce.
3. Add shredded cheese to the egg and spices mixture.
4. Pour 1 tbsp. shredded cheese in a waffle maker and cook for 30 sec.
5. Pour Chaffles batter in the waffle maker and close the lid.
6. Cook chaffles for about 4 minutes Utes until crispy and brown.
7. Carefully remove chaffles from the maker.
8. Serve on the bed of spinach with boil egg, avocado slice, and tomatoes.

---

9. Enjoy!

Nutrition: Protein: 23% 77 kcal Fat: 66% 222 kcal
Carbohydrates: 11% 39 kcal

Morning Chaffles With Berries

Preparation: 10 minutes | Cooking: 5 Minutes | Servings: 4

Ingredients

- 1 cup egg whites
- 1 cup cheddar cheese, shredded
- ¼ cup almond flour
- ¼ cup heavy cream

Topping:

- 4 oz. raspberries
- 4 oz. strawberries.
- 1 oz. keto chocolate flakes
- 1 oz. feta cheese.

Directions

1. Preheat your square waffle maker and grease with cooking spray.
2. Beat egg white in a small bowl with flour.
3. Add shredded cheese to the egg whites and flour mixture and mix well.
4. Add cream and cheese to the egg mixture.
5. Pour Chaffles batter in a waffle maker and close the lid.
6. Cook chaffles for about 4 minutes Utes until crispy and brown.
7. Carefully remove chaffles from the maker.
8. Serve with berries, cheese, and chocolate on top.
9. Enjoy!

Cauliflower & Italian Seasoning Chaffles

Preparation: 10 minutes | Cooking: 20 Minutes | Servings: 2

Ingredients
- 1 cup cauliflower rice
- ¼ teaspoon garlic powder
- ½ teaspoon Italian seasoning
- Salt and freshly ground black pepper, to taste
- ½ cup Mexican blend cheese, shredded
- 1 organic egg, beaten
- ½ cup Parmesan cheese, shredded

Directions
- Preheat a mini waffle iron and then grease it.
- In a blender, add all the ingredients except Parmesan cheese and pulse until well combined.
- Place 1½ tablespoon of the Parmesan cheese in the bottom of preheated waffle iron.
- Place ¼ of the egg mixture over cheese and sprinkle with the ½ tablespoon of the Parmesan cheese.
- Cook for about 4-minutes or until golden brown.
- Repeat with the remaining mixture and Parmesan cheese.
- Serve warm.

Nutrition: Calories 58, Fat 5.2, Fiber 1.2, Carbs 2.7, Protein 1.1

Chaffle & Chicken Lunch Plate

Preparation: 5 Minutes | Cooking: 15 Minutes | Servings: 1

Ingredients
- 1 large egg
- 1/2 cup jack cheese, shredded
- 1 pinch salt

For Serving:
- 1 chicken leg
- salt
- pepper
- 1 tsp. garlic
- 1 egg
- I tsp avocado oil

Directions
1. Heat your square waffle maker and grease with cooking spray.
2. Pour Chaffle batter intothe skillet and cook for about 3 minutes.
3. Meanwhile,heat oil in a pan, over medium heat.
4. Once the oil is hot, add chicken thigh and garlicthen, cook for about 5 minutes. Flip and cook for another 3-4 minutes.
5. Season with salt and pepper and give them a good mix.
6. Transfer cooked thigh to plate.
7. Fry the egg in the same pan for about 1-2 minutes according to your choice.

---

8. Once chaffles are cooked, serve with fried egg and chicken thigh
9. Enjoy!

Nutrition: Protein: 31% 138 Kcal, Fat: 66% 292 Kcal, Carbohydrates: 2% Kcal

Keto Blt Chaffle Sandwich

Preparation: 5 Minutes | Cooking: 15 Minutes | Servings: 4

Ingredients
- 1/2 cup mozzarella shredded
- 1 egg
- 1 tbs green onion diced
- 1/2 tsp Italian seasoning

Sandwich Ingredients:
- Bacon pre-cooked
- Lettuce
- Tomato sliced
- 1 tbs mayo

Directions
1. Preheat the mini waffle maker
2. In a small bowl, whip the egg.
3. Add the cheese, seasonings, and onion. Mix it until it's well incorporated.
4. Place half the batter in the mini waffle maker and cook it for 4 minutes.
5. If you want a crunchy bread, add a tsp of shredded cheese to the mini waffle iron for 30 seconds before adding the batter. The extra cheese on the outside creates the best crust!
6. After the first chaffle is complete, add the remaining batter to the mini waffle maker and cook it for 4 minutes.

7. Add the mayo, bacon, lettuce, and tomato to your sandwich.
8. Enjoy!

Nutrition: Protein: 38% 121 Kcal, Fat: 59% 189 Kcal, Carbohydrates: 3% 11 Kcal

Bacon Cheddar Bay Biscuits Chaffle Recipe

Preparation: 5 Minutes | Cooking: 6 Minutes | Servings: 6

Ingredients

- 1/2 cup Almond Flour
- 1/4 cup Oat Fiber
- 3 strips of bacon cooked and crumbled
- 1 Egg, beaten
- 1/4 cup Sour Cream
- 1 T Bacon Grease melted
- 1 1/2 tbsp Kerrygold Butter melted
- 1/2 cup Sharp Cheddar Cheese shredded
- 1/2 cup Smoked Gouda Cheese shredded
- 1/4 tsp Swerve Confectioners
- 1/2 tsp Garlic Salt
- 1/2 tsp Onion Powder
- 1/2 tbsp Parsley dried
- 1/2 tbsp Baking Powder
- 1/4 tsp Baking Soda

Directions

1. Preheat mini waffle maker.
2. Mix almond flour, baking powder, baking soda, onion powder, and garlic salt to a bowl and mix using a whisk.

3. In another bowl, add the eggs, bacon, sour cream, parsley, bacon grease, melted butter, and cheese. Mix until combined.
4. Add the dry ingredients into the wet and mix.
5. Scoop 2-3 T of the mix into hot waffle iron and cook for 5-6 minutes.

Nutrition: Total Fat 12.5g, Total Carbohydrate 4.3g, Protein 7.7g

Chaffle Burger

Preparation: 5 minutes | Cooking: 10 Minutes | Servings: 2

Ingredients

For the burger:

- 1/3-pound ground beef
- ½ tsp garlic salt
- 2 slices American cheese

For the chaffles:

- 1 large egg
- ½ cup shredded mozzarella
- ¼ tsp garlic salt
- For the sauce:
- 2 tsp mayonnaise
- 1 tsp ketchup
- 1 tsp dill pickle relish
- splash vinegar, to taste

For the toppings:

- 2 Tbsp shredded lettuce
- 3-4 dill pickles
- 2 tsp onion, minced

Directions

- Heat a griddle over medium-high heat.
- Divide ground beef into balls and place on the griddle, 6 inches apart. Cook for 1 minute.
- Use a small plate to flatten beef. Sprinkle with garlic salt.

- Cook for 2-3, until halfway cooked through. Flip and sprinkle with garlic salt.
- Cook for 2-3 minutes, or until cooked completely.
- Place cheese slice over each patty and stack patties. Set aside on a plate. Cover with foil.
- Turn on waffle maker to heat and oil it with cooking spray.
- Whisk egg, cheese, and garlic salt until well combined.
- Add half of the egg mixture to waffle maker and cook for 2-3 minutes.
- Set aside and repeat with remaining batter.
- Whisk all sauce ingredients in a bowl.
- Top one chaffle with the stacked burger patties, shredded lettuce, pickles, and onions.
- Spread sauce over the other chaffle and place sauce side down over the sandwich.
- Eat immediately.

Nutrition: Calories 206, Fat 6.2, Fiber 3.6, Carbs 7.9, Protein 8.6

Broccoli Chaffles

Preparation: 6 minutes | Cooking: 8 Minutes | Servings: 2

Ingredients

- 1/3 cup raw broccoli, chopped finely
- ¼ cup Cheddar cheese, shredded
- 1 organic egg
- ½ teaspoons garlic powder
- ½ teaspoons dried onion, minced
- Salt and freshly ground black pepper, to taste

Directions

1. Preheat a mini waffle iron and then grease it.
2. In a medium bowl, place all ingredients and, mix until well combined.
3. Place ¼ of the mixture into preheated waffle iron and cook for about 4 minutes or until golden brown.
4. Repeat with the remaining mixture.
5. Serve warm.

Nutrition: Calories 123, Fat 2.9, Fiber 2.2, Carbs 7.5, Protein 4.3.

Asparagus Chaffle

Preparation: 10 minutes | Cooking: 15 minutes | Servings: 4

Ingredients

- 4 eggs
- 1½ cups grated Mozzarella cheese
- ½ cup grated parmesan cheese
- 1 cup boiled asparagus, chopped Salt and pepper to taste
- ¼ cup almond flour
- 2 teaspoons baking powder
- 2 tablespoons cooking spray to brush the waffle maker ¼ cup Greek yogurt for serving
- ¼ cup chopped almonds for serving

Directions

1. Preheat the waffle maker.
2. Add the eggs, grated mozzarella, grated parmesan, asparagus, salt and pepper, almond flour and baking powder to a bowl.
3. Mix with a fork.
4. Brush the heated waffle maker with cooking spray and add a few tablespoons of the batter.
5. Close the lid and cooking for about 7 minutes depending on your waffle maker.
6. Serve each chaffle with Greek yogurt and chopped almonds.

Nutrition: Calories 400, Fat 15, Fiber 4, Carbs 25, Protein 14

Rosemary Pork Chops on Chaffle

Preparation: 10 minutes | Cooking: 15 minutes | Servings: 4

Ingredients

- 4 eggs
- 2 cups grated Mozzarella cheese Salt and pepper to taste
- Pinch of nutmeg
- 2 tablespoons sour cream
- 6 tablespoons almond flour
- 2 teaspoons baking powder
- Pork chops
- 2 tablespoons olive oil
- 1 pound pork chops
- Salt and pepper to taste
- 1 teaspoon freshly chopped rosemary
- 2 tablespoons cooking spray to brush the waffle maker
- 2 tablespoons freshly chopped basil for decoration

Directions

1. Preheat the waffle maker.
2. Add the eggs, Mozzarella cheese, salt and pepper, nutmeg, sour cream, almond flour and baking powder to a bowl.
3. Mix until combined.
4. Brush the heated waffle maker with cooking spray and add a few tablespoons of the batter.
5. Close the lid and cooking for about 7 minutes depending on your waffle maker.

---

6. Meanwhile, heat the butter in a nonstick grill pan and season the pork chops with salt and pepper and freshly chopped rosemary.
7. Cooking the pork chops for about 4-5 minutes on each side.
8. Serve each chaffle with a pork chop and sprinkle some freshly chopped basil on top.

Nutrition: Calories 236, Fat 12, Fiber 2, Carbs 7, Protein 15

Chaffle With Cream Cheese Frosting

Preparation: 5 Minutes | Cooking: 6 Minutes | Servings: 6

Ingredients

- 1 egg
- 1/2 cup mozzarella cheese
- 1/2 tsp pumpkin pie spice

Cream Cheese Frosting:

- 2 tbs cream cheese softened and room temperature
- 2 tbs monk fruit confectioners blend or any of your favorite keto-friendly sweetener
- 1/2 tsp clear vanilla extract

Directions

1. Preheat the waffle maker.
2. In a small bowl, whip the egg.
3. Add the cheese and pumpkin pie spice
4. Mix well.
5. Add 1/2 of the mixture to the mini waffle maker and cook it for at least 3 to 4 minutes until it's golden brown.
6. While the chaffle is cooking, add all of the cream cheese frosting ingredients in a bowl and mix it until it's smooth and creamy.
7. Add the cream cheese frosting to the hot chaffle and serve it immediately.

Nutrition: Calories 84, Total Fat 4.5g, Total Carbohydrate 5.3g, Protein 6.1g

Zucchini Nut Bread Chaffle Recipe

Preparation: 8 Minutes | Cooking: 15 Minutes | Servings: 5

Ingredients

- 1 small zucchini, shredded
- 1 egg
- 1/2 teaspoon cinnamon
- 1 Tbsp plus 1 tsp erythritol blend such as Swerve, Pyure or Lakanto
- Dash ground nutmeg
- 2 tsp melted butter
- 1 ounce softened cream cheese
- 2 tsp coconut flour
- 1/2 tsp baking powder
- 3 tablespoons chopped walnuts or pecans

Frosting:

- 2 ounces cream cheese at room temperature
- 2 Tbsp butter at room temperature
- 1/4 tsp cinnamon
- 2 Tbsp caramel sugar-free syrup such as Skinny Girl, or 1 Tbsp confectioner's sweetener, such as Swerve plus 1/8 tsp caramel extract
- 1 Tbsp chopped walnuts or pecans

Directions

1. Grate zucchini and place in a colander over a plate to drain for 15 minutes. With your hands, squeeze out as much moisture as possible.
2. Preheat waffle iron until thoroughly hot.

3. In a medium bowl, whisk all chaffle ingredients together until well combined.
4. Spoon a heaping 2 tablespoons of batter into waffle iron, close and cook 3-5 minutes, until done. Remove to a wire rack. Repeat 3 times.

Frosting:

1. Mix all ingredients together until smooth and spread over each chaffle. Top with additional chopped nuts.
2. Serve and Enjoy!

Nutrition: Total Fat 5.5g, Total Carbohydrate 1.8g, Protein 6.8g

Bbq Chicken Chaffle

Preparation: 3 minutes | Cooking: 8 minutes | Servings: 2

Ingredients

- 1/3 cup cooked chicken diced
- 1/2 cup shredded cheddar cheese
- 1 tbsp sugar-free bbq sauce
- 1 egg
- 1 tbsp almond flour

Directions

1. Heat up your mini waffle maker.
2. In a small bowl, mix the egg, almond flour, BBQ sauce, diced chicken, and Cheddar Cheese.
3. Add 1/2 of the batter into your mini waffle maker and cook for 4 minutes. If they are still a bit uncooked, leave it cooking for another 2 minutes. Then cook the rest of the batter to make a second chaffle.
4. Do not open the waffle maker before the 4 minute mark.
5. Enjoy alone or dip in BBQ Sauce or ranch dressing!

Nutrition: Calories: 205kcal, Carbohydrates: 2g, Protein: 18g, Fat: 14g

Keto Tuna Melt Chaffle Recipe

Preparation: 15 minutes | Cooking: 8 minutes | Servings: 2

Ingredients

- 1 packet Tuna 2.6 oz. with no water
- 1/2 cup Mozzarella cheese
- 1 egg
- pinch salt

Directions

1. Preheat the mini waffle maker
2. In a small bowl, add the egg and whip it up.
3. Add the tuna, cheese, and salt and mix well.
4. Optional step for an extra crispy crust: Add a teaspoon of cheese to the mini waffle maker for about 30 seconds before adding the recipe mixture. This will allow the cheese to get crispy when the tuna chaffle is done cooking. I prefer this method!
5. Add 1/2 the mixture to the waffle maker and cooking it for a minimum of 4 minutes.
6. Remove it and cooking the last tuna chaffle for another 4 minutes.

Nutrition: Calories 283, Fat 20.2, Fiber 3.3, Carbs 1.4, Protein 14.5

Raspberry & Custard Chaffle

Preparation: 5 minutes | Cooking: 55 minutes | Servings: 2 chaffles

Ingredients

For Chaffles

- 1 tbsp almond flour
- ½ cup mozzarella cheese
- 1 egg, beaten
- 1 tbsp sweetener
- ½ tsp vanilla extract

For Custard:

- 2 eggs
- 2 tbsp heavy cream
- 1 tbsp brown sugar substitute
- ½ tsp cinnamon powder
- ½ tsp vanilla extract

For Topping:

- 2 tbsp of fresh raspberries

Directions

For Custard:

1. Preheat the oven at 350 °.
2. Now, place all ingredients in a small bowl and stir until well combined.

3. Pour the mixture in a baking tin and bake it for about 40-45 min.
4. Now, remove from heat and set aside to cool.

For Chaffles:

5. Heat up the waffle maker.
6. Add all the chaffles ingredients to a small mixing bowl and combine well.
7. Pour ½ of the batter into your waffle maker and cook for 4 minutes until golden brown. Then cook the remaining batter to make another chaffle.
8. Top the chaffles with custard and sprinkle with raspberries.
9. Serve and enjoy!

Delicious Chaffle

Preparation: 5 minutes | Cooking: 55 minutes | Servings: 2 chaffles

Ingredients

For Chaffles:

- ½ cup shredded mozzarella cheese
- 1 tbsp almond flour
- 1 egg, beaten
- ¼ tsp cinnamon
- ½ tbsp sweetener
- 2 tbsp low carb chocolate chips

For Custard:

- 2 eggs
- 2 tbsp heavy cream
- 1 tbsp brown sugar substitute
- ½ tsp cinnamon powder
- ½ tsp vanilla extract

Directions

Directions for custard:

1. Preheat the oven at 350°.
2. Place all your ingredients in a small bowl and stir until well combined.
3. Pour the mixture in a baking tin and bake it for about 40-45 min.
4. Now, remove from heat and set aside to cool.

Directions for chaffles:

5. Heat up the waffle maker.
6. Add all the chaffles ingredients to a small mixing bowl and combine well.
7. Pour ½ of the batter into your waffle maker and cook for 4 minutes until golden brown. Then cook the remaining batter to make another chaffle.
8. Top the chaffles with custard.
9. Serve and enjoy!

Yogurt Chaffle & Blueberries

Preparation: 5 minutes | Cooking: 8 minutes | Servings: 2 chaffles

Ingredients

- ½ cup mozzarella cheese, shredded
- 1 egg, beaten
- 1 tbsp yogurt
- 1 tbsp fresh blueberries, chopped
- ¼ tsp baking powder

Directions

1. Heat up the waffle maker.
2. Now, add all the ingredients to a tiny mixing bowl and stir until well combined.
3. Pour now half of the batter into the waffle maker and cook for 4 minutes until it is brown. Repeat with the rest of the batter to prepare another chaffle.
4. Serve and enjoy!

Strawberry Yogurt Chaffle

Preparation: 5 minutes | Cooking: 8 minutes | Servings: 2 chaffles

Ingredients

- ½ cup mozzarella cheese, shredded
- 1 egg, beaten
- 1 tbsp yogurt
- 1 tbsp fresh strawberries, chopped
- ¼ tsp baking powder

Directions

1. Heat up the waffle maker.
2. Add all your ingredients to a small mixing bowl and stir until well combined.
3. Pour half of the batter into your waffle maker and cook for 4 minutes until brown. Repeat now with the rest of the batter to prepare another chaffle.
4. Serve and enjoy!

Vanilla Chaffle with Lemon Icing

Preparation: 5 minutes | Cooking: 8 minutes | Servings: 2 chaffles

Ingredients

For Chaffles

- 1 tbsp almond flour
- ½ cup mozzarella cheese
- 1 egg, beaten
- 1 tbsp sweetener
- ½ tsp vanilla extract

For Lemon Icing:

- 2 tbsp powdered erythritol
- 4 tsp heavy cream
- 1 tsp lemon juice
- Lemon zest

Directions

1. Heat up the waffle maker.
2. Add all the ingredients for the chaffles to a small mixing bowl and combine well.
3. Pour ½ of the batter into your waffle maker and cook for 4 minutes. Then cook the remaining batter to make another chaffle.
4. Combine in a mixing bowl the powdered erythritol, heavy cream, lemon juice and lemon
5. zest.
6. Pour over vanilla chaffle. Serve and enjoy!

Macadamia Nuts Chaffle

Preparation: 5 minutes | Cooking: 8 minutes | Servings: 2 chaffles

Ingredients

- 1 tbsp almond flour
- ½ cup mozzarella cheese, shredded
- 1 egg, beaten
- 1 tbsp sweetener
- ½ tsp vanilla extract
- A pinch of salt
- 1 tbsp Macadamia nuts, minced

Directions

1. Heat up the waffle maker.
2. Now, add all the ingredients to a small mixing bowl and combine well.
3. Pour ½ of the batter into your waffle maker and cook for 4 minutes until golden brown. Then cook the remaining batter to make another chaffle.
4. Top the chaffles with keto whipped cream.
5. Serve and enjoy!

Lightning Source UK Ltd.
Milton Keynes UK
UKHW020646140621
385483UK00011B/555